DAWNING LIGHT
PERSPECTIVES ON FRIENDSHIP

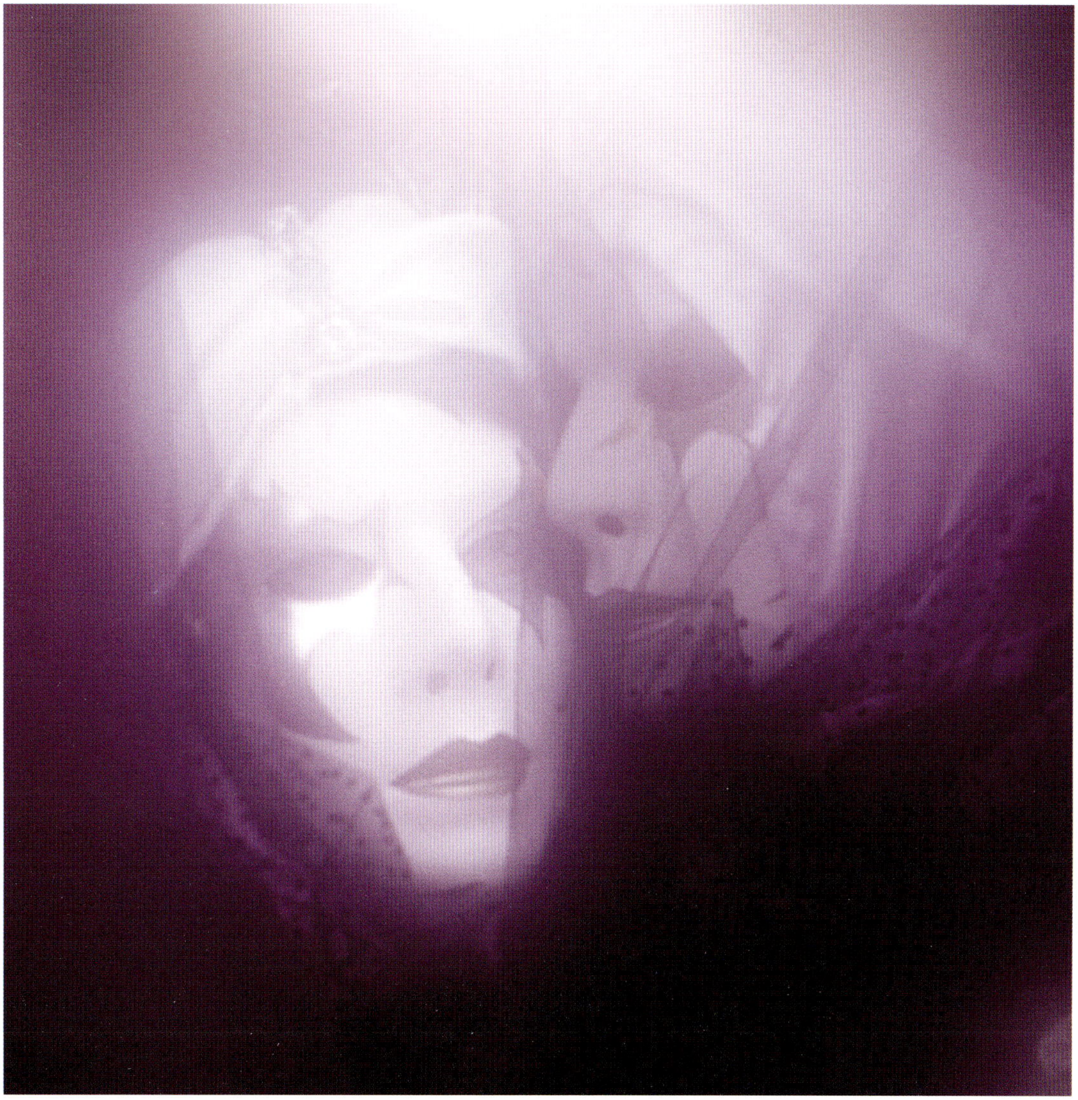

The poetry of DAVID TONG and
the photography of PETER KARRY

*We dedicate this book
to the memory of our mutual school friend,
Keith Jeffery,
who died in a tragic swimming accident
shortly after our happy reunion.*

DAWNING LIGHT
David Tong and Peter Karry

Published in the UK by Arem Publishing Ltd

British Library Cataloguing-in-Publication Data:
A catalogue record for the book is available from the British Library.

ISBN 1-904825-05-2
First edition, 2005

Design and production management by Arem Publishing Ltd, England.
Printed in Italy by Graphic Studio, Verona.

Introduction

In July 1960 two boys left school. Each had done well academically at Queen Elizabeth's Grammar School in Ashbourne, Derbyshire. University degrees and successful, rewarding careers followed: Peter Karry via insurance to IT Alliances Director with ICL; and David Tong via medical school to Consultant Clinical Oncologist at Guy's Hospital. Contact was lost, but friendship made in those formative years would survive. So in 1998 when these school friends were reunited they still found much in common, in spite of 38 years on different paths.

They each possess an artistic ability of which the other was unaware – Peter in photography and David in poetry. The subsequent mutual respect and admiration was to strengthen the bond of friendship and led to a desire to cooperate in this joint publication.

Peter has enjoyed considerable success as an amateur photographer, his individual style and unique perspective winning national competitions and resulting in many images being published in books and journals such as *Practical Photography* and *Konica Minolta Photoworld*.

David's poetry was written for family, friends, colleagues and patients to provide amusement, comfort and hope. Several poems have been published in *GKT* (formerly known as *Guy's Gazette*) – the world's oldest hospital journal. David's poetic philosophy is perfectly described in the first poem, *Dawning Light*, which provided the title for this book.

Although their artistic expression takes very different forms, both share the same values and derive the same pleasure from the beauty of nature and the warmth of humanity. Their art flows from deep within, formed from the magma of education, experience and family background to emerge and crystallise in beautiful words and pictures. This small, intimate collection was selected from considerable portfolios of poems and photographs to commemorate friendship in its many guises.

It has been my privilege to assist my old school friends, Peter and David, in assembling this book and a great honour to have been asked to provide the introduction.

Ian Hood

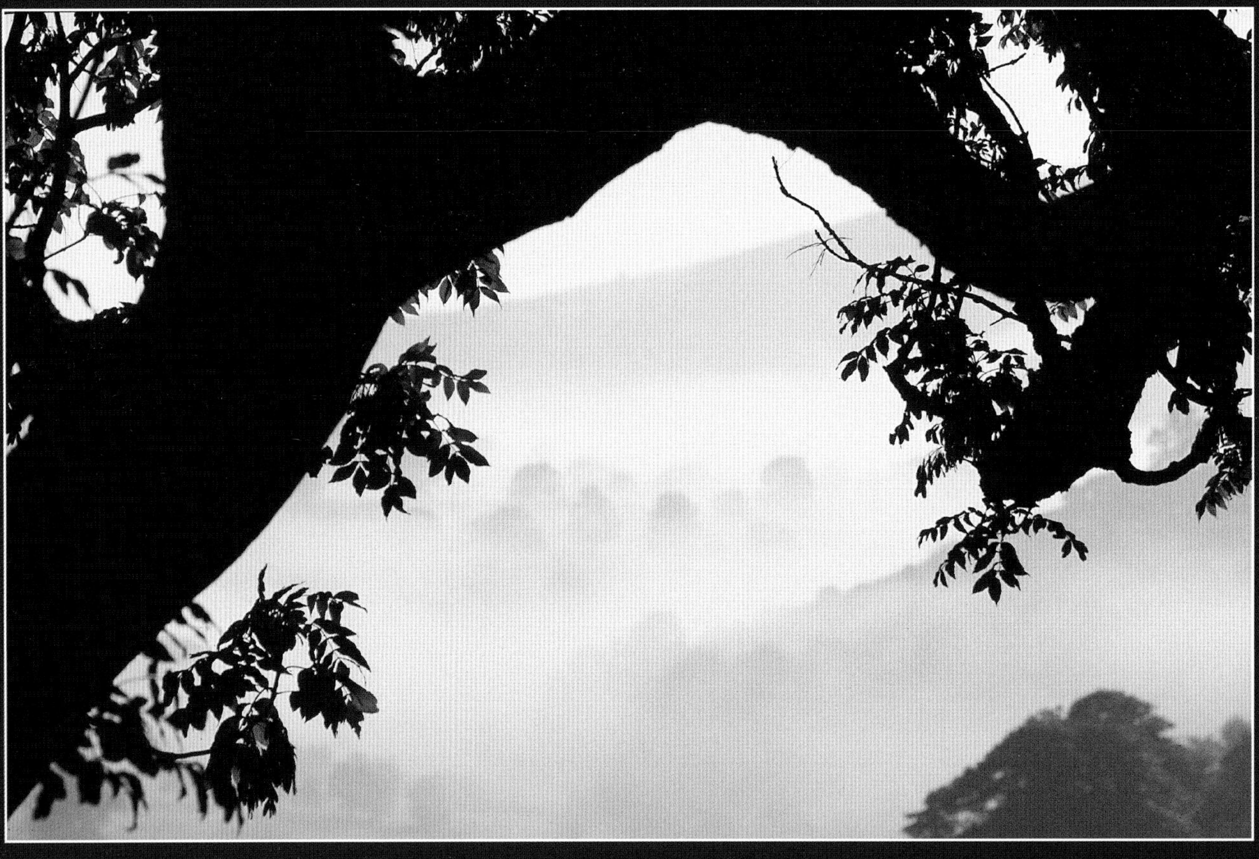

Dawning Light

I have never been trained in Art
Or studied Literature.
My words come, simply, from the heart
Uncomplicated, naïve but pure.

I believe that verse should be like song
And gently flow like rivers out to sea
And carry thoughts, like flowers, along
Like the sentiments that flow from me.

Poems should be like the evening tide
And ebb and flow across the beach.
Not like the pure water locked inside
Deep wells, cool and dark and out of reach.

I think that noble verse should rhyme
And, like measured foot prints in the sand,
Be like music in a structured time
So that even humble folk can understand.

Verse should be like dawn light through the trees
To illuminate, with that inner sound
And carry life's music with simplicity
Even if the message is profound.

Invitation to the Dance

Take my hand and cross the darkened ballroom,
I will guide you through the dancing crowds.
Press into my arms and let our love bloom;
Let us dance above the clouds.

Let us dance as if no tomorrow;
Let us dream to those familiar songs;
Let us forget the pains and sorrows;
Let us dance the whole night long.

Let us forget those tired limbs,
Blind to the strands of greying hairs,
Let us toss our faces in the winds
And dance together up the marble stairs.

We have passed our waltzing prime
But, we have trod the paths where Strauss has been.
Our hearts can still beat in three-quarter time;
Take my hand, come share my dreams.

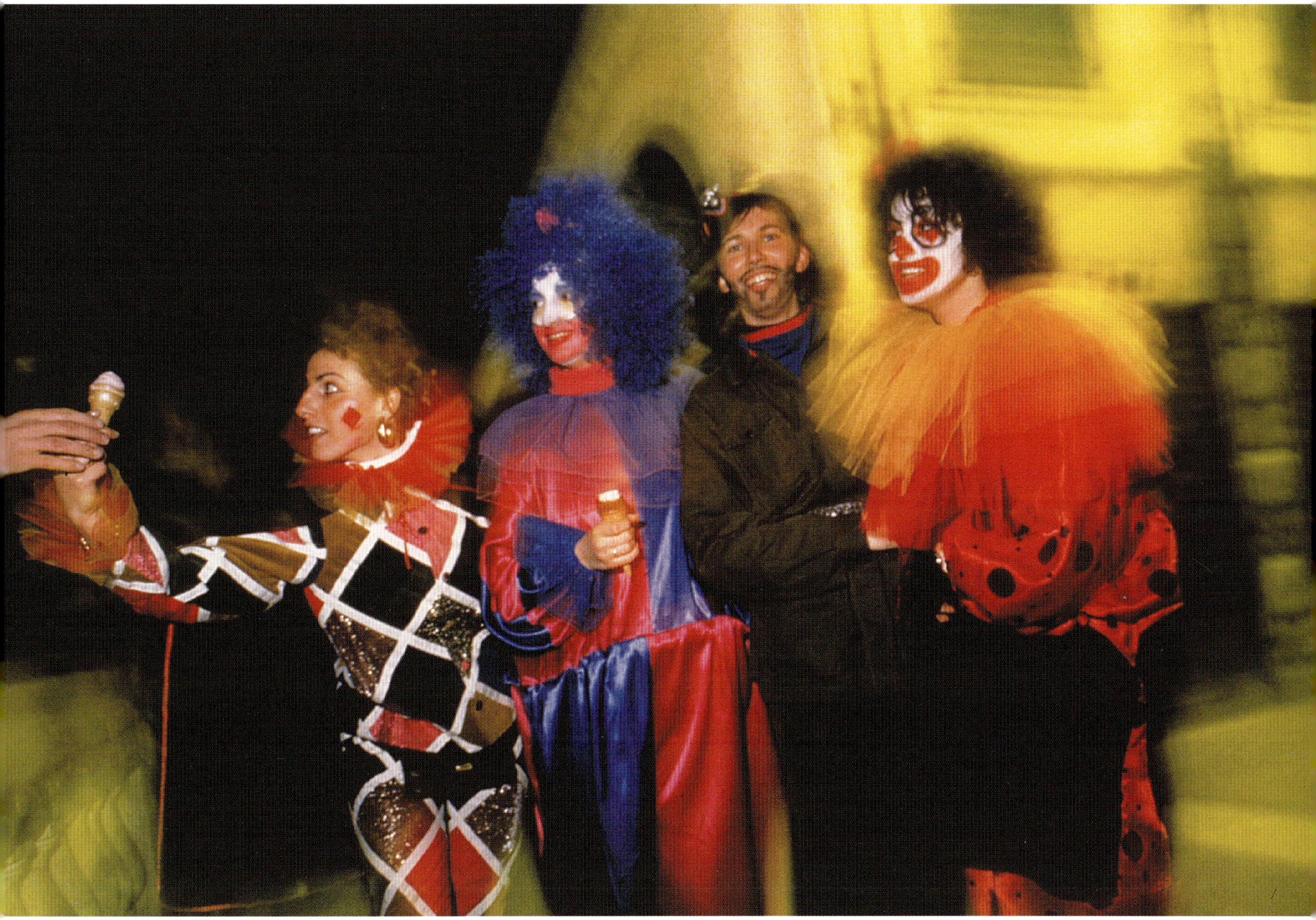

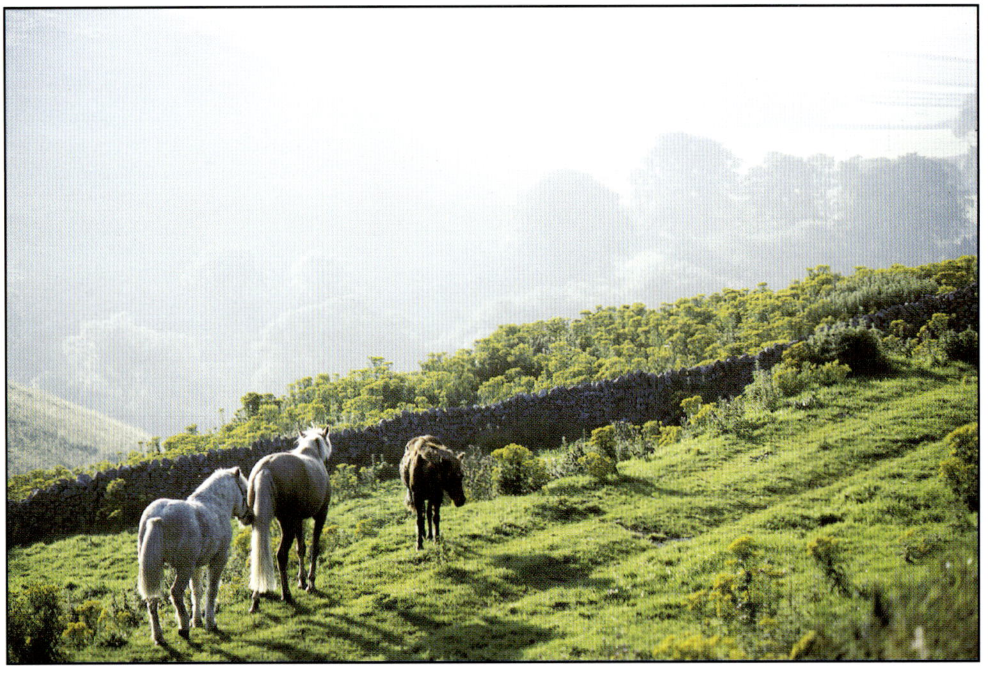

Summer Meadows

I recall that warm day in my native Derbyshire,
When the bright colours dripped out of summer skies;
When the swathes of golden buttercups caught fire
And drowsy meadows droned to hum of bees and flies.

We walked in warm contentment through the long, lush grass;
Through the clammy moistness which brushed upon our thighs.
The panting, trusty dogs would, sometimes, amble past
When skylarks, from their shy obscurity would rise.

We heard the larks rise, effortlessly, on the rungs
Of those unseen ladders in the blue, cloudless skies.
Their notes embossed on our memories and flung,
At random, like the dandelion seeds fly.

We lay back amongst the buttercups and savoured
Such a day, when man and dog and sky were just one.
But, such sweet memories leave a bitter flavour:
The meadows and the panting dogs have long since gone.

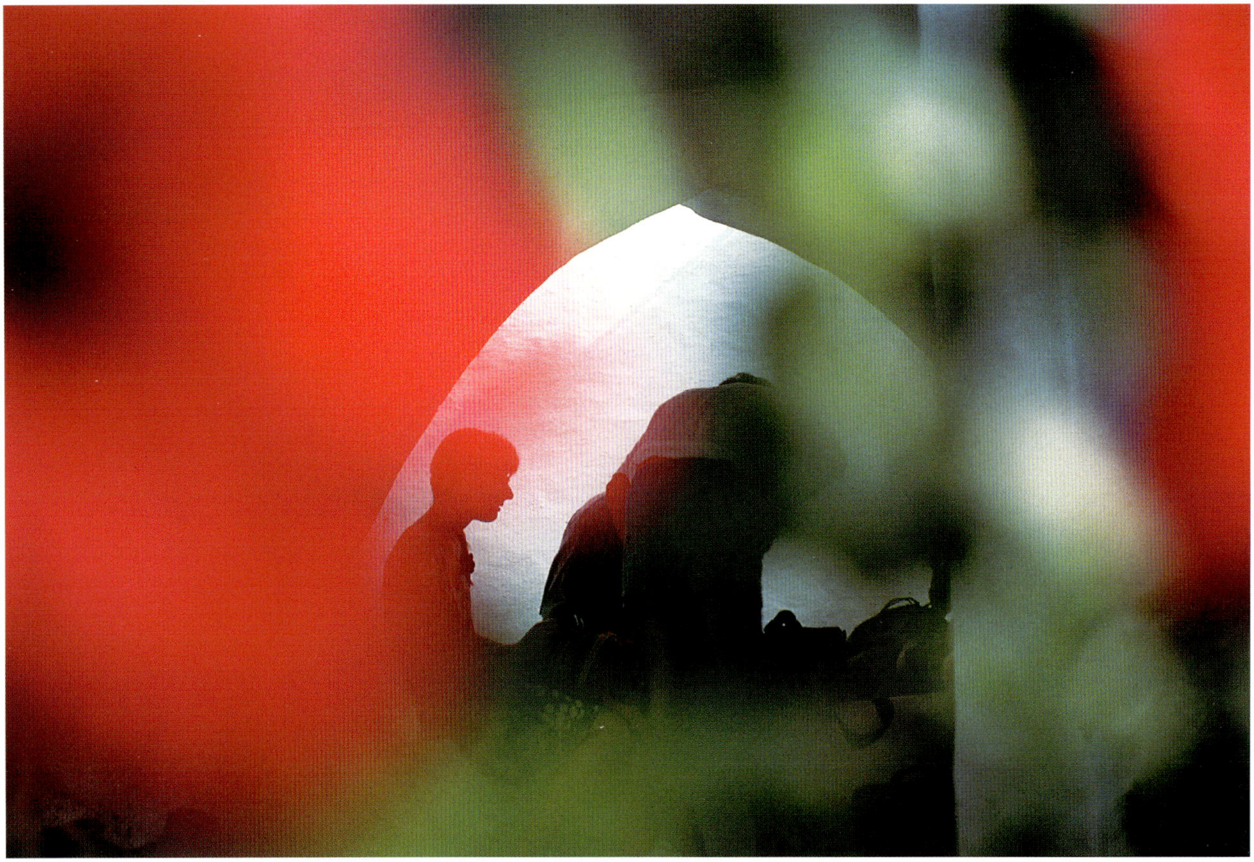

Ambience

How good it is, with friends, to sit and dine;
To sup; to share their special ambience;
To inhale the rich bouquets of wines;
To slip into that warm, seductive trance.
How comforting to gaze into the glass
And share the glint of warm reflections;
To hear the lazy talk as hours pass;
To taste laughter; the meal's rich selections.
How satisfying are those bites of food;
The tit-bits of the friendly conversations;
The shared morsels of thought that can be chewed
Around the palate with delectation.
O what warmth is there to sup with friends
And what mellow thoughts each mouthful sends.

Freundschaft

I did not understand the words he spoke
But I saw friendship within his eyes;
Those eyes of honest, country folk,
Like clear, cloudless, summer skies.

He offered not just a glass of beer,
But a welcome in his huge, rustic hand;
An iron grip; eyes equally sincere,
That strangers could not fail to understand.

We were ushered to a rough-hewn bench
That sat beside a solid table.
Then downed the beer, a thirst to quench,
But only as fast as custom would enable.

We watched the friendly conversations;
Tried to unravel the animated jokes.
We felt that we would suffer isolation
As only German words were spoke.

But, we felt at ease amongst the friends;
Shining eyes cast in our direction
And, without words, they tried to send
Their cheers, glasses raised with warm affection.

Here, in the warmth of the Hessen hills;
In the embrace of Mittel German sun,
No words were needed to keep cups filled
And to make the flowing friendship come.

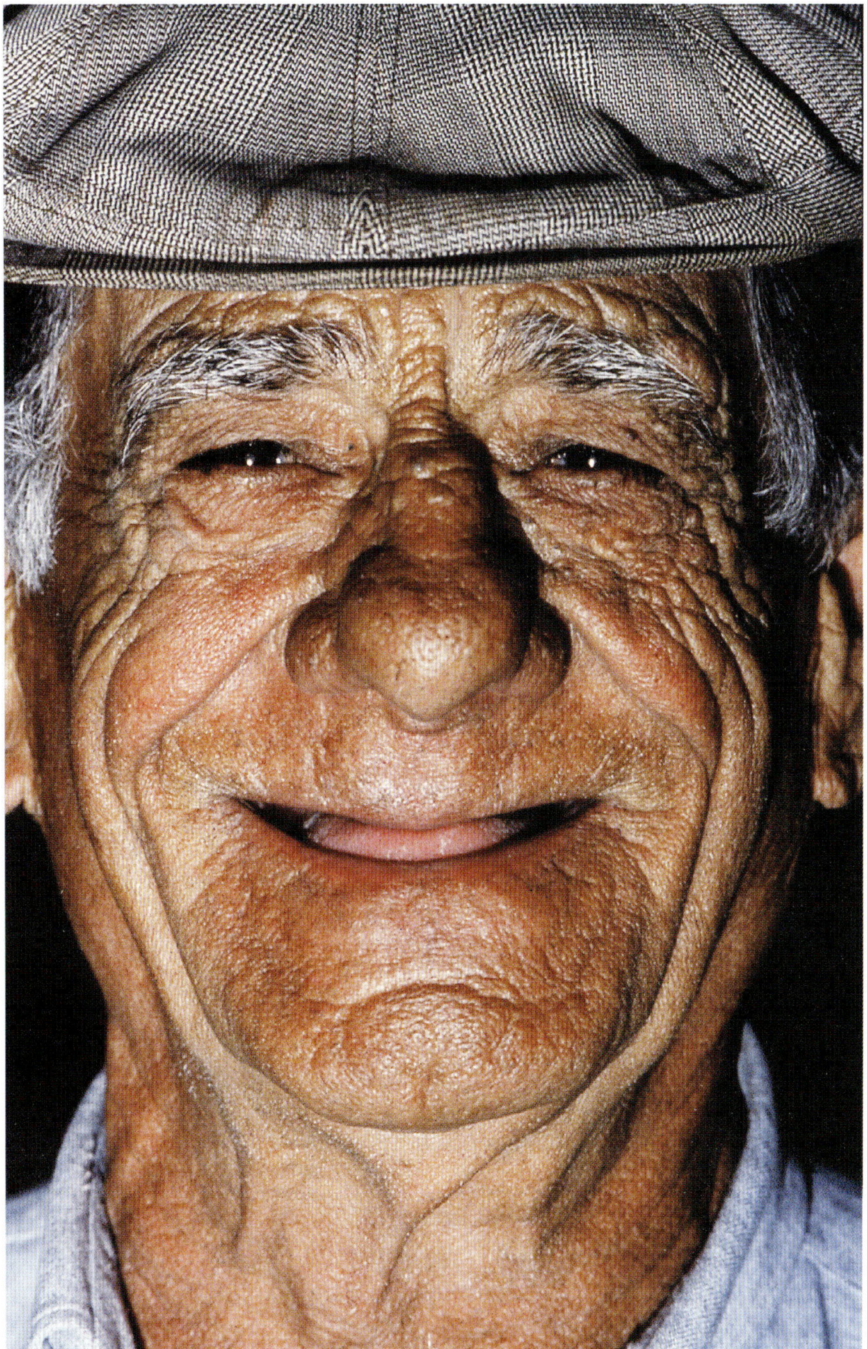

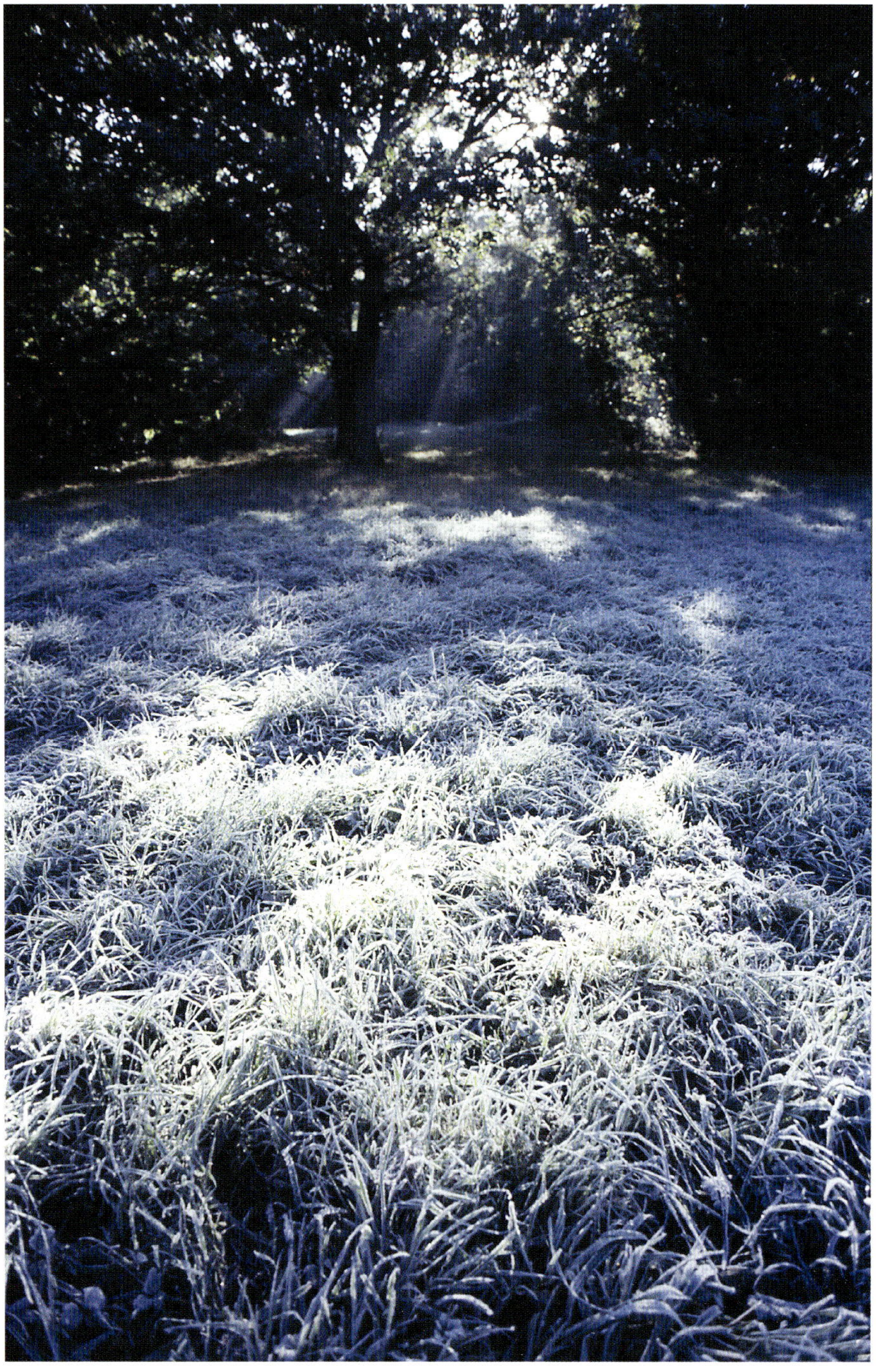

Let Sleeping Dogs Lie

How I long for my faithful dogs
When we stretched together by the fireside logs.
How I miss those warm canine sighs
As we dozed together with sleepy eyes.
And watched the light of glowing embers
On frosty nights in late November.
How I miss the breaths upon my hand
And the electric response if I should stand.
O that I could stretch from my fireside seat
And feel the weight of dogs across my feet.
Or reach out and touch that rugged coat
Then hear that contented growl within the throat.
How I yearn for that conjoint sleep
As man and dog the vigil keep.
On a long and cold December night
When the winter fire is burning bright.
O that I could feel that other warmth
That the love of a sleeping dog can spawn.

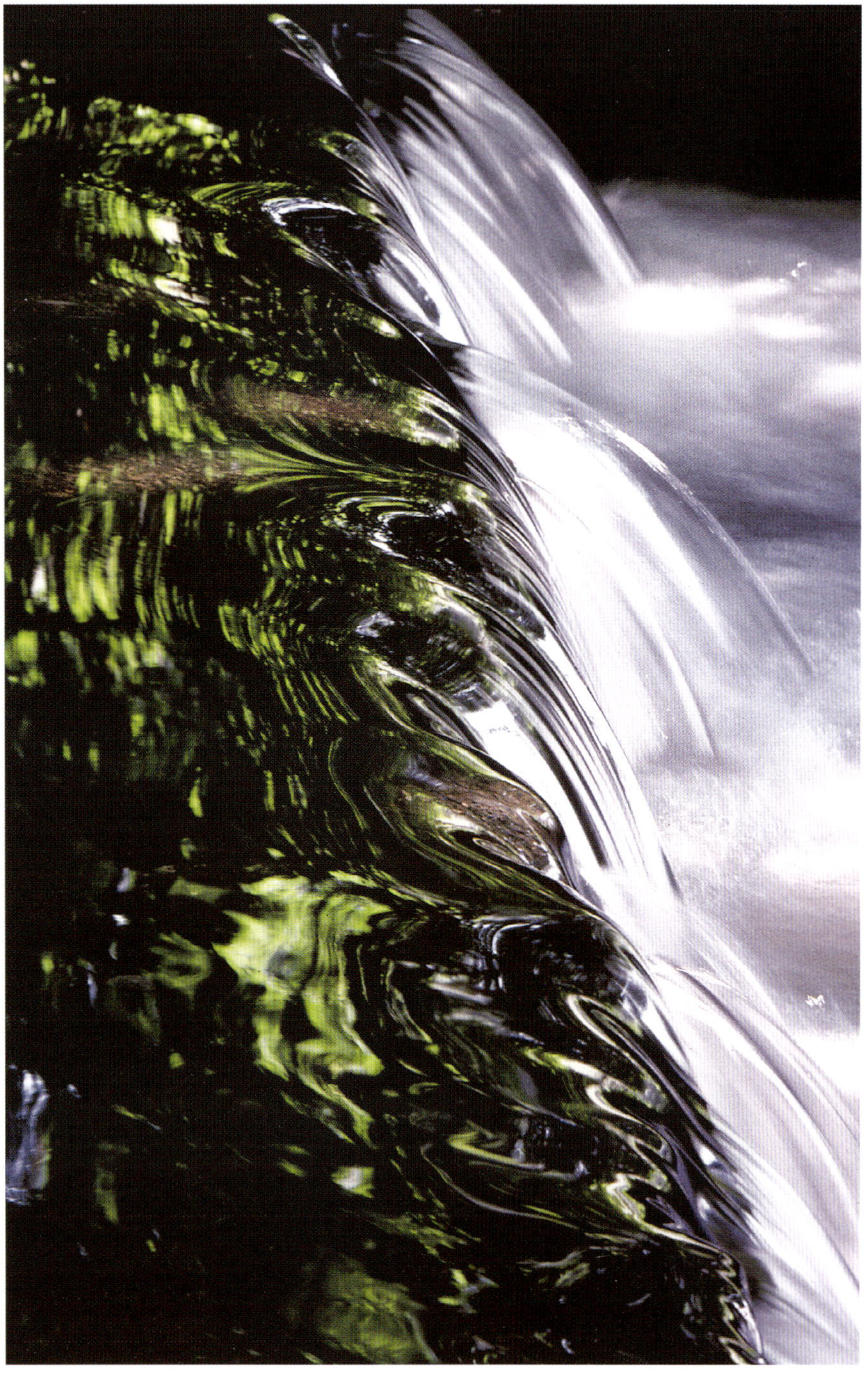

Rivers of Memories

How good it was to hear the cold Dove talk;
To hear the quick, white-breasted dippers sing;
To share, with special friends, that Dovedale walk
And hear the carillons of mem'ry ring.
What depth those icy ripples seemed to reach.
They plunged into the hollows of recall.
How quickly we lapsed into schoolboy speech,
In bubbling, Derbyshire waterfalls.
We realised that years could not erase
Or wash away those sediments of time.
Those cherished memories of schoolboy days
Were trapped, like the coral within the lime.
We were the children of Izaak Walton's sons,
Where his beloved, limestone river runs.

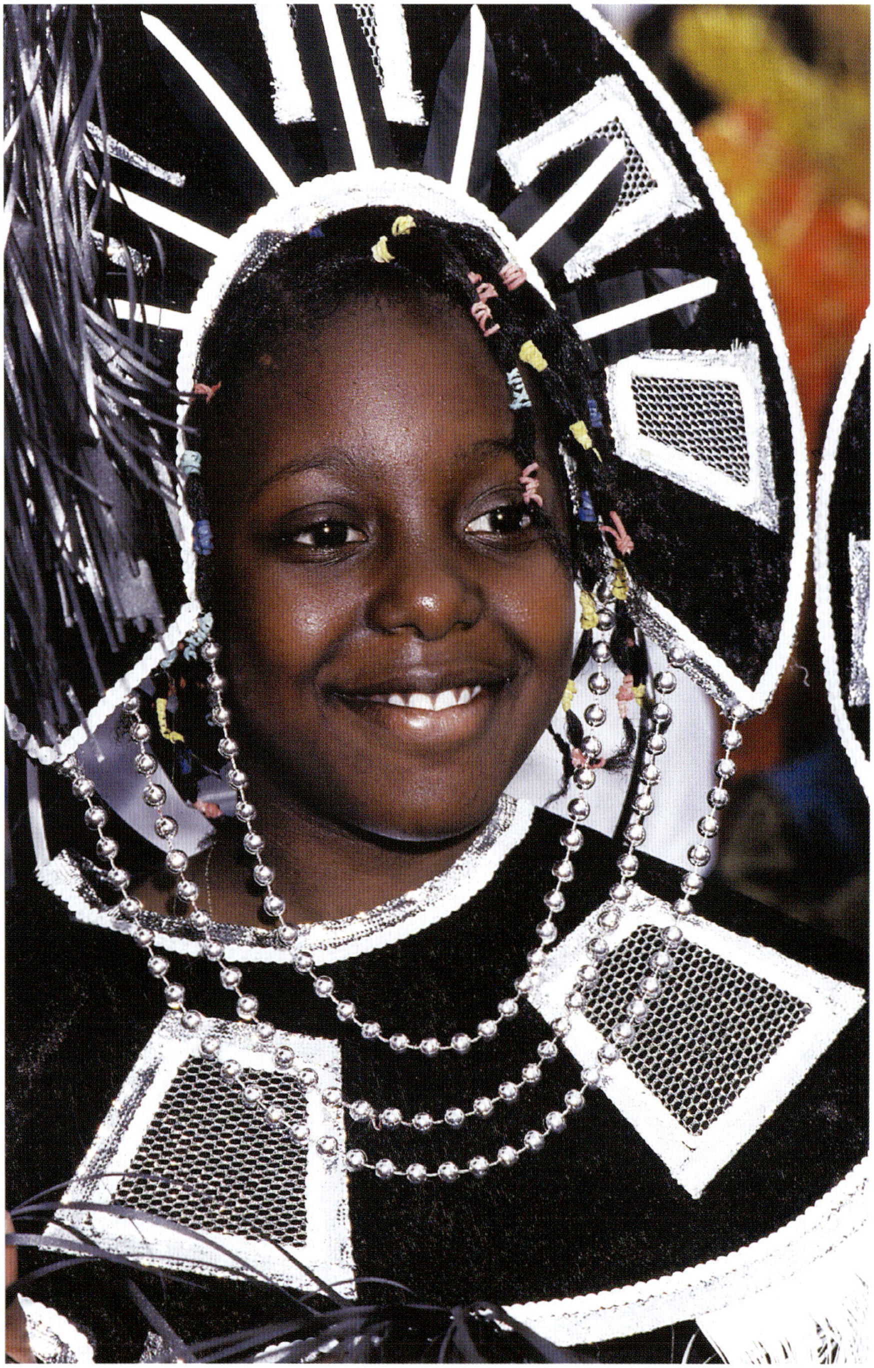

Anatomy of a Smile

A smile
Is that brief spark of recognition
Across a floor of strangers;
A smile is that quiet smirk
Of the stranger on the train
With the dog-eared book on the knee.
A smile is that bright-eyed gratitude
Of the child as the paper is pulled back
From a large, coloured box.
A smile is the meaningful glance
Of the demure lover.
A smile is that concealed mirth
Of the first two rows of pupils
As the schoolmaster turns round to show his shirt flap.
A smile is that joyous greeting
As you open the draughty door and see a friend.
A smile is that restful satisfaction
As you lay on the pillow after that final goodnight kiss.
A smile is that explosion of love and recognition
In the eyes of a baby.

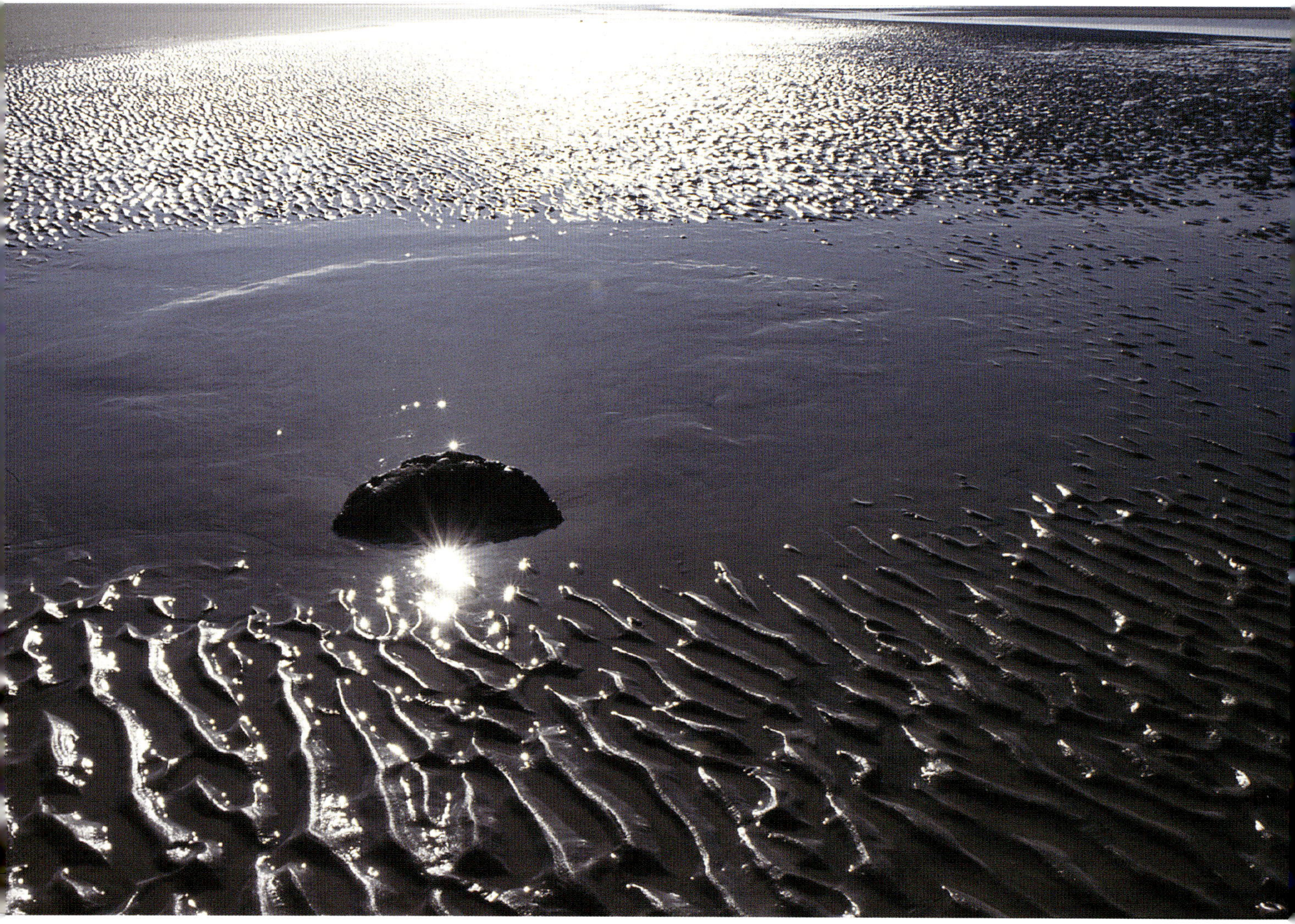

Tears in the Sand

They did not build funeral pyres for thee.
No noble poet shed tears in the sand,
Nor laid your ashes in a cemetery
In the soft, green shade of a foreign land.
They did not etch your name on gates of time;
No white-haired mason carved your name in stone;
No fly-leaf tears before your epic lines;
No revered sepulchre in ancient Rome.
No, dear friend, I will shed my private tears
Of when they plucked your body from the sea
But, I will be comforted by those years
And the words and friendship you shared with me.
This humble epitaph that I set down
Is to our long friendship: it did not drown.

Reflections on a Wet Autumn Day

Forgive me, friend, I could not sing for you.
I could not sing those anthems and rejoice
For a life we shared and to say adieu:
The jaws of grief gripped hard; I had no voice.

Forgive me, friend, I could not see the words
Of the carefully chosen hymns of praise.
My welling tears made the lines seem blurred;
The image of you hid them from my gaze.

Forgive me, friend, that I cannot recall
The words others spoke in their eulogies.
They were like watching winter snowflakes fall:
They melted in my own warm memories.

Forgive me, friend, that I did not extend
My hand to touch your family or your wife.
That it did not reach out, forgive me, friend:
I was in another world; another life.

Forgive me, friend, that I did not see your face
Or kneel by your noble ashes at the end.
That I did not give you a warm embrace
When we last said farewell, please forgive me, friend.

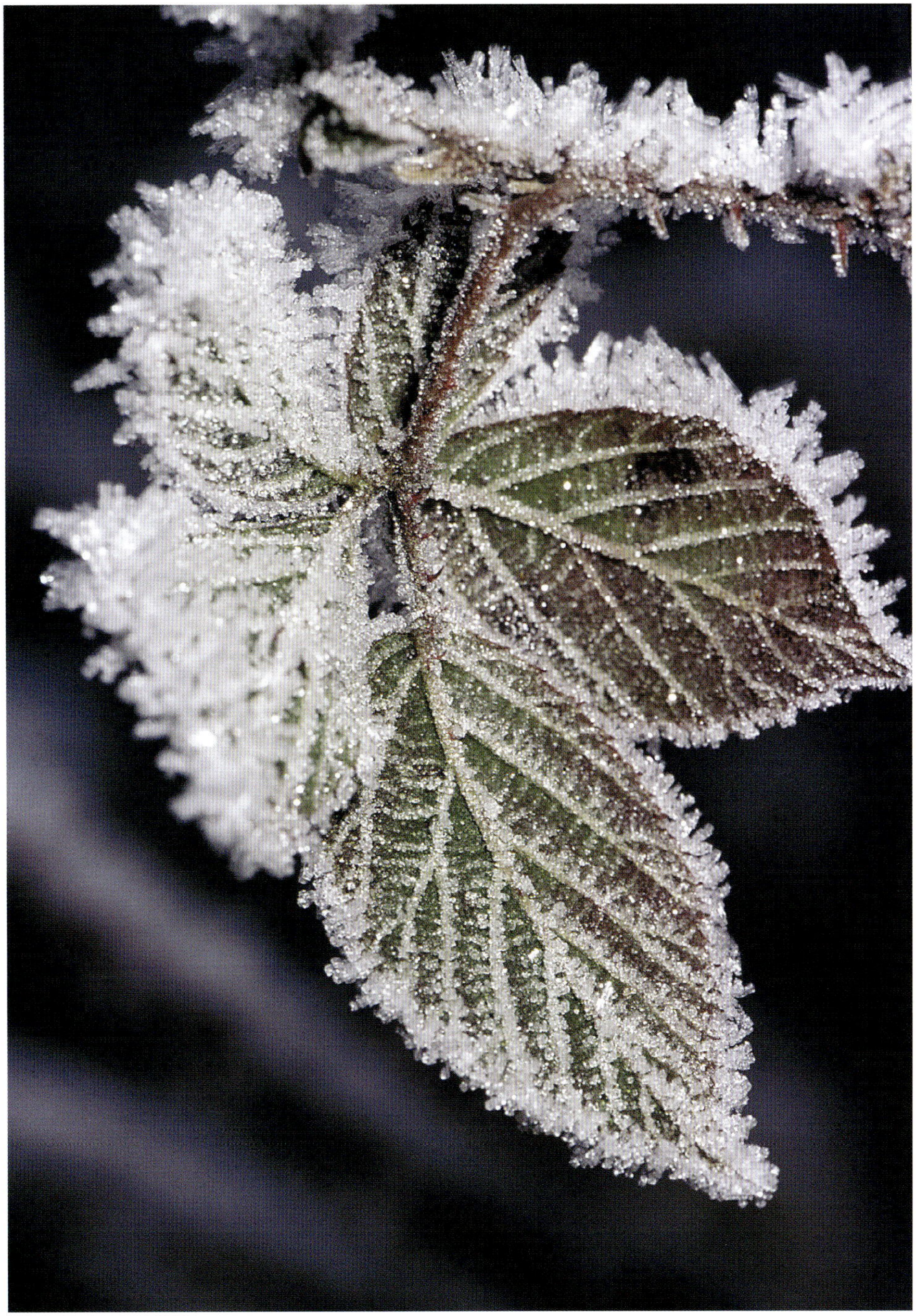

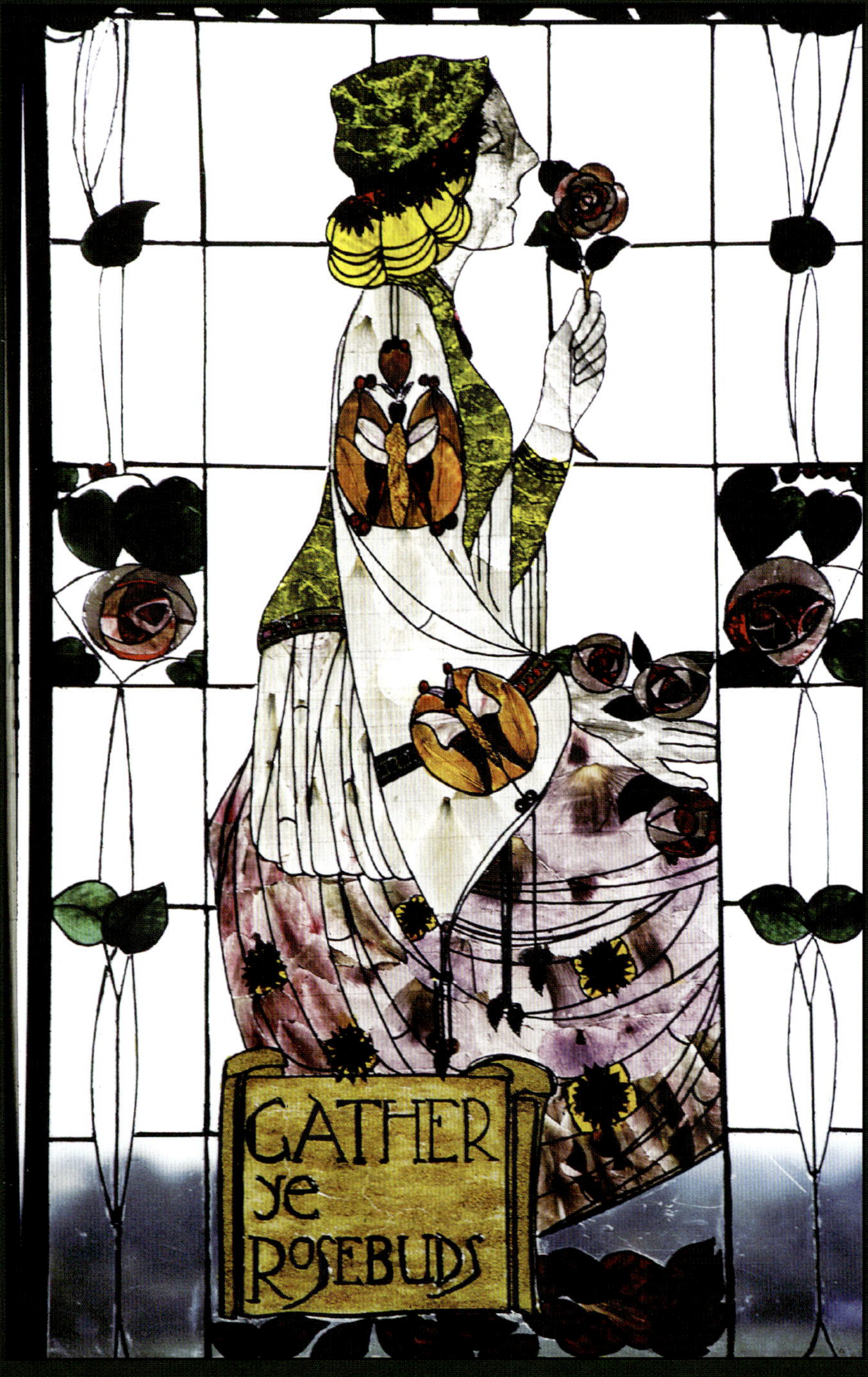
GATHER
YE
ROSEBUDS

Cherished Memories

O Olive, who will speak of thee?
Who will mourn your quiet passing?
You have out-lived your family;
'Tis the young who now count their blessings.
You stood by your own daughter's grave
And by those of husband and of kin;
Those hard roads with which life is paved
And made your journey long and grim.
But, you had no bitter thoughts;
No regrets where you had trod.
You said those things you had been taught
And those things you learned from life and God.
You held out a welcome hand,
To neighbours and to poor relations.
You showed a gift to understand,
And to engage in conversation.
You survived with wheezy breaths;
You lived through wars and injuries;
You comforted those touched by death
And tears of a whole century.
You watched me grow from infancy;
As school-boy, student and as a man.
You were a quiet constancy
Of my own, mere six decade span.
Now, you are but an old man's dream;
Soon, a hazy recollection,
But you will live in my esteem
And be a keystone of my affections.
You gazed from windows of me at play,
To ensure I would not come to harm.
I now gaze at those flower bouquets,
Which lie there in deathly funeral calm.
I had so many things still to say;
So many questions of the past,
But, dear aunt, I can only pray
That my cherished memories will e'er last.

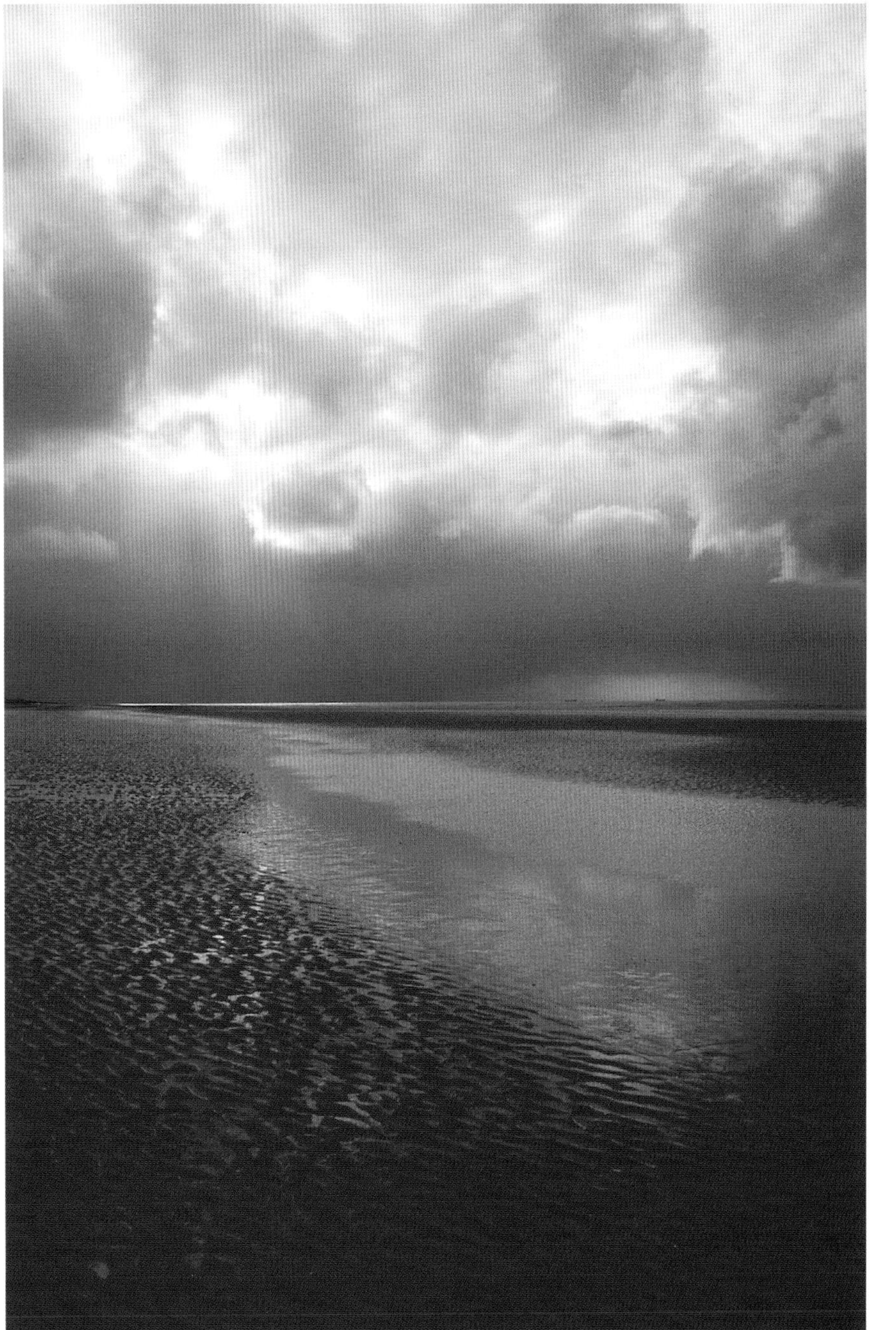

Summer Tides

We sat there in the shallow waters
And felt the tide wash past our feet,
Still enveloped in the dreams that brought us
To where the warm sands and the cold seas meet.

We sat there, dreaming, at the shore-line
To music that from quiet oceans seeps:
The hiss of summer tides that ebbed in time
Like the soft expirations of gentle sleep.

We saw the frothing sea run 'cross our fingers
And sat there steeped in bubbles and the brine.
We watched the dark stains where the tide had lingered
On those warm idyllic sands of time.

O that such magic could last for ever
And, from storms of life we could always hide.
That, from such warmth we could not be severed,
And we could sit, always, in the summer tides.

Attributes of Love

You are both my rock and precious stone,
You are the summer breeze upon my face.
You are the winter fire when I come home;
You are my sanctuary of warm embrace.
You are the scent of rose upon the wind.
You are the essence of my soothing balm.
You are my lover, sister and my friend.
You are the grace that keeps our house from harm.
You are the glowing ember in my fire.
You are that refreshing sip of water.
You are the quenching pool of my desires.
You are the mother of my son and daughters.
Can you be all these wondrous things to me
Yet real flesh and blood, not poetry?

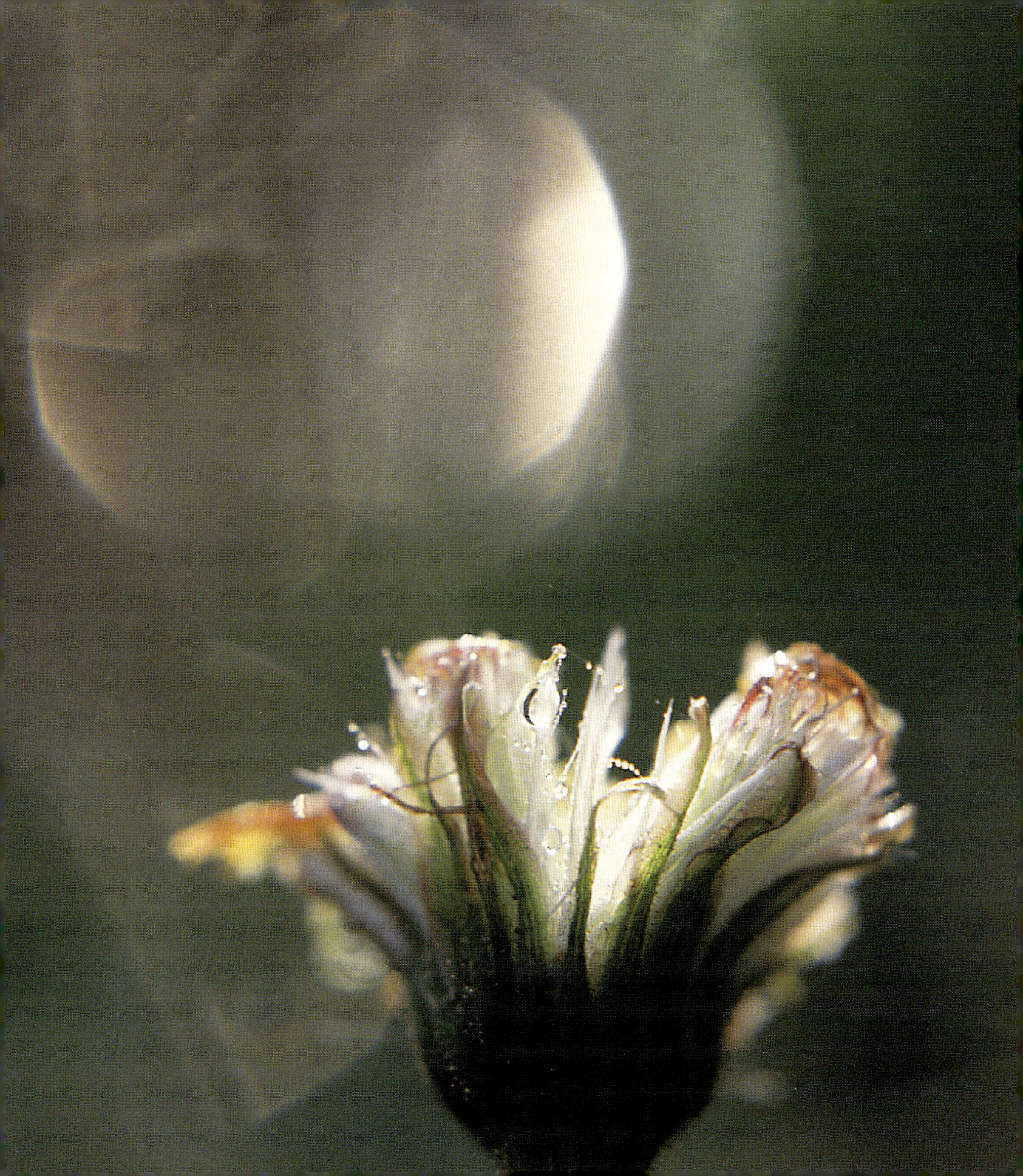

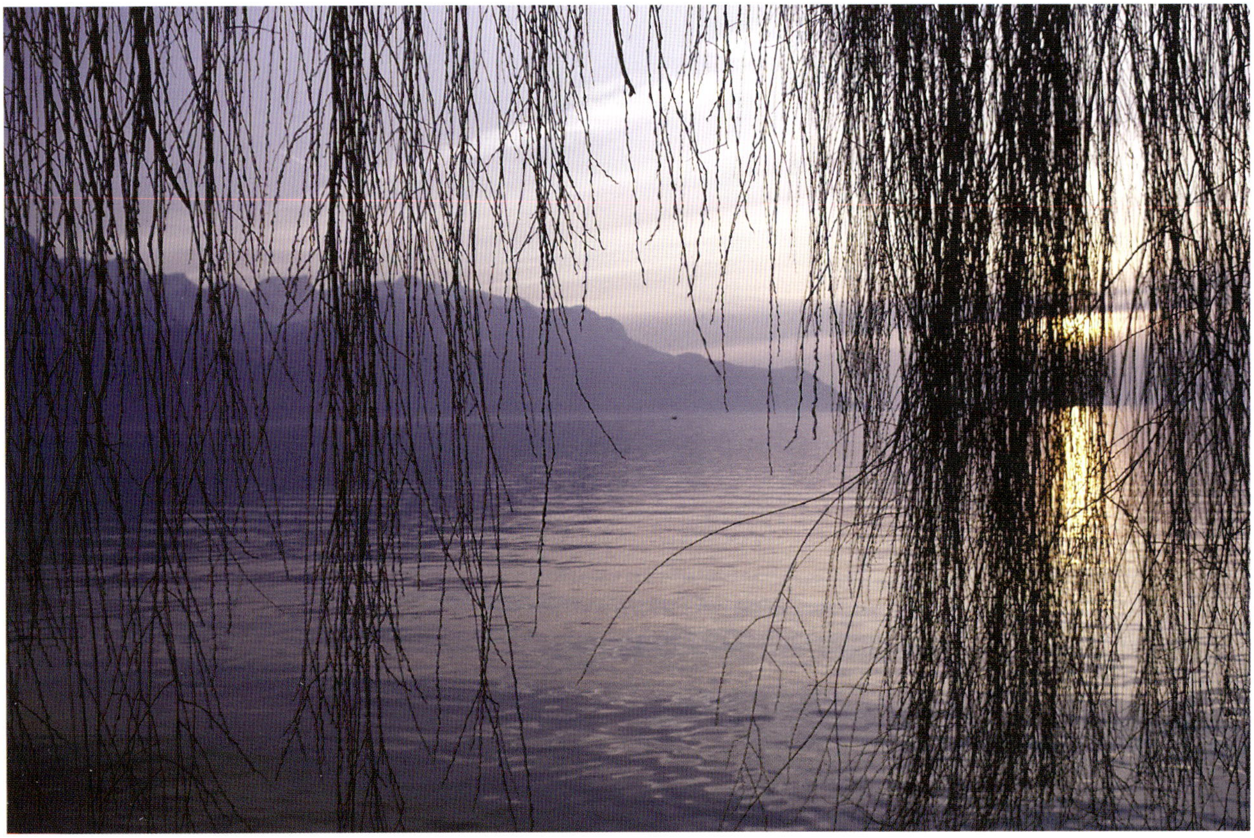

Willow

Should I compare thee to a willow tree:
Hanging, tall and languid, in the summer sun?
Calm and proud, full of warm serenity,
As those fingers drape, where cool rivers run.
Could I capture your style, your elegance,
If I stood there, beneath that tranquil shade?
Those pleasant years, that slipped past like a trance
And still glow as the autumn sunlight fades.
How I will miss that dappled sanctuary:
The murmur of mellow conversations;
The quiet seclusion you gave to me;
That slender image, my consolation.
May those warm memories always linger,
In my rivers, where you trailed your fingers.

Games of Life

Dear friend, when I peruse that frail frame-work
On which our brief and humble lives are draped,
I thank God for that chance, that wondrous quirk,
Which made our own paths cross and take shape.
How blessed are we, that when the dice were tossed,
They rolled with faces in our direction.
What richness, what pleasures would I have lost,
Should one die have failed, by chance deflection.
O that I could perceive this game of chance;
That I knew the outcomes of the shaker.
But, if I knew destiny, in advance,
Would I share divine schemes of our Maker?
I know not how or why those fortunes spilled
But may our friendship last and be fulfilled.

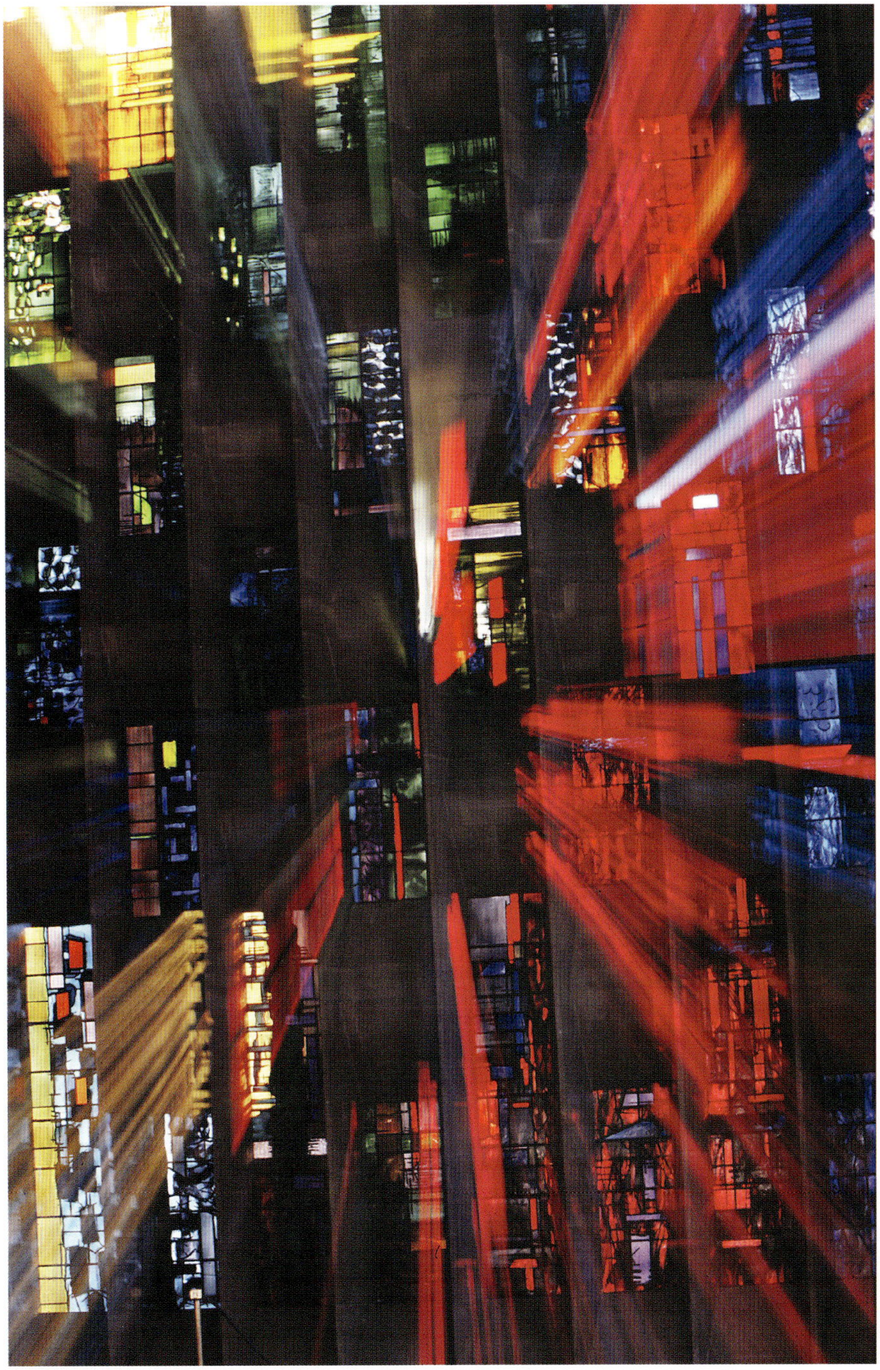

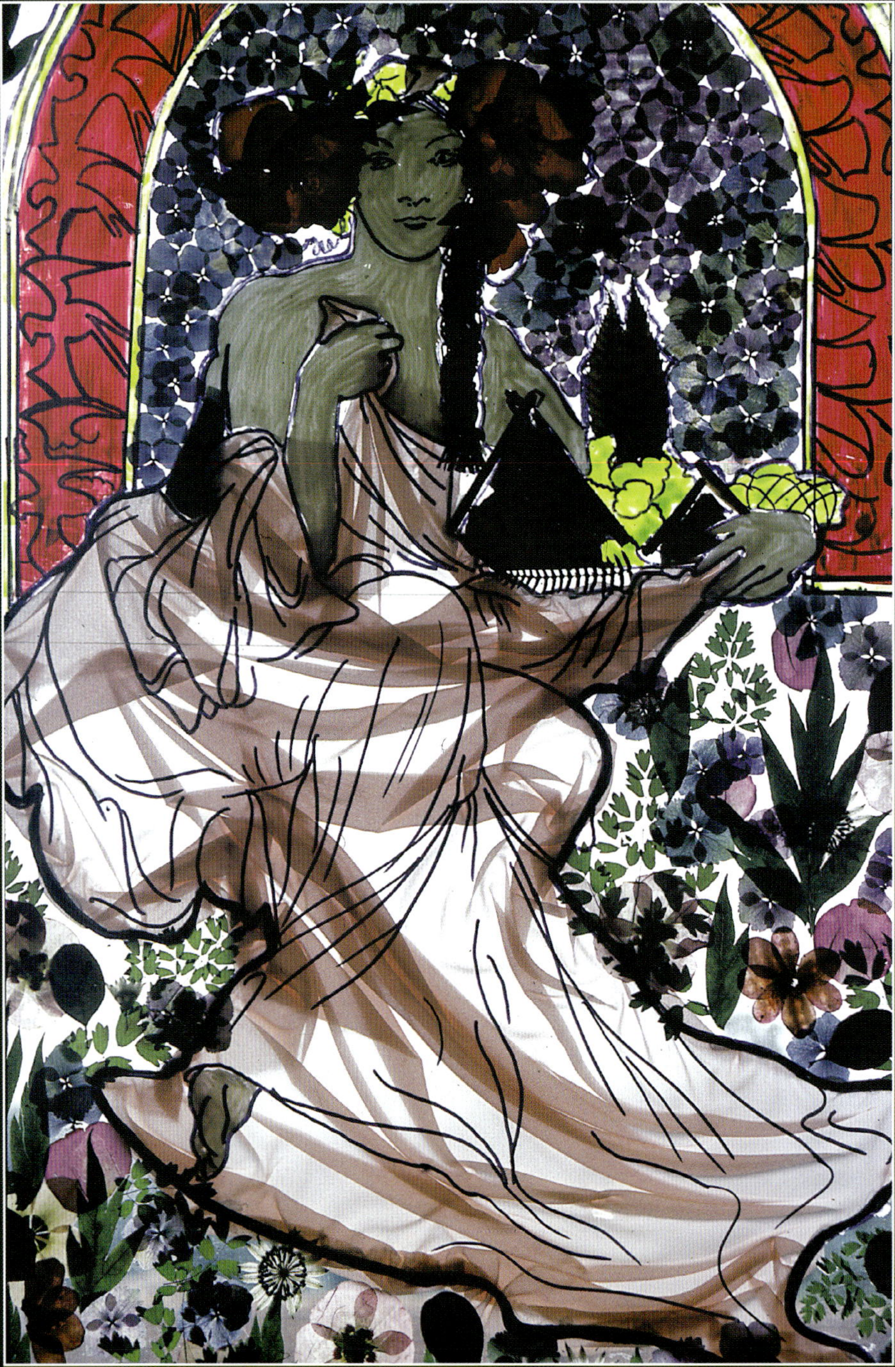

Concern

There are times when we need to touch friends' souls;
When our gestures and sweet words seem hollow;
Days when their skies go dark and thunder rolls
And we pray for the peace which, later, follows.
They see pain in our eyes and our concern;
Our own reticence to show our feelings.
How can they know that flames inside us, burn
For them, and dance, bright, on our ceilings.
They cannot feel that warmth of inner fire;
The hot embers, as we rake thoughts' ashes
They cannot know the flames that they inspire,
Which no storm, no cloud-burst, ever dashes.
That bright, eternal flame inside us burns,
Behind our worried frowns and our real concerns.

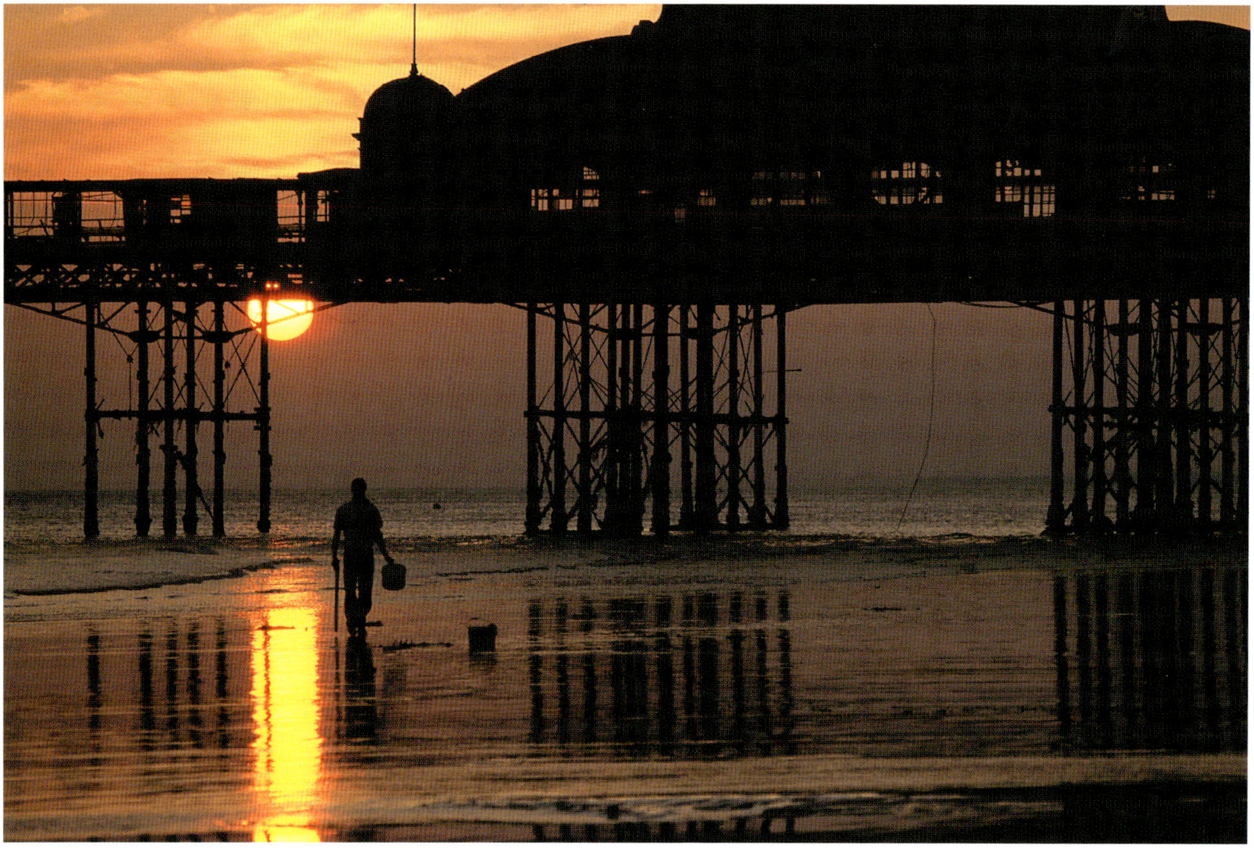

Dolphin Schools

There are times when you see just black despair;
When you seem a rock in a sea of tears;
When few in a heartless world seem to care;
When, even sleep, does not blot out your fears.
You may feel you struggle against the tides
And dark currents, in the endless oceans;
When you experience no warmth inside
And your soul has run dry of all emotion.
Remember, your friends are there around you,
Like friendly dolphins in clear, shallow seas.
We will support you, on gleaming backs of blue
And carry you to warm, safe sanctuaries.
You may not see us; we have no outstretched hands,
But we are there around you: we understand.

Lighthouse Keepers

O dearest light-beam, Patient B,
What a tower of strength you have been to me.
You have faced more pain, more threat than I,
But always with a smile; a twinkle in the eye.
'Tis I who should have lead the way,
Over rocky paths, where few can stray
But you held the lantern, silently,
To show that track I could not see.
With your shining light and quiet courage,
You gave inspiration when I felt discouraged.
You showed that distant goals are quite possible,
By small steps, inch by inch; your role immeasurable.
I have reached the foothills of my final goal
And I have you to thank for your quiet role.
'Tis now the time to pass the lamp once more
And, for me, to find us a lighthouse even more secure.
I have nought but praise and thanks to offer thee,
O brave and smiling, Patient B.

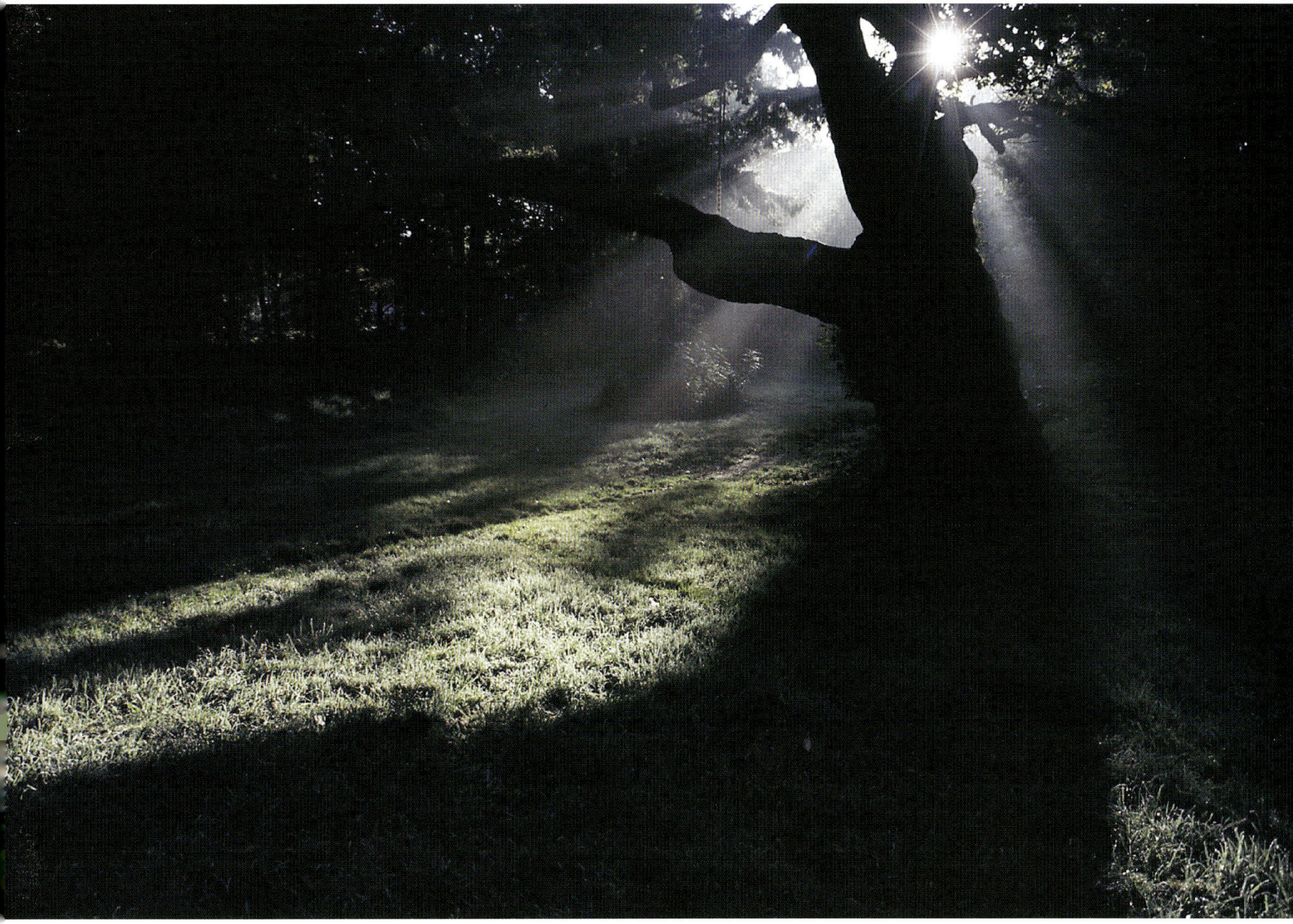

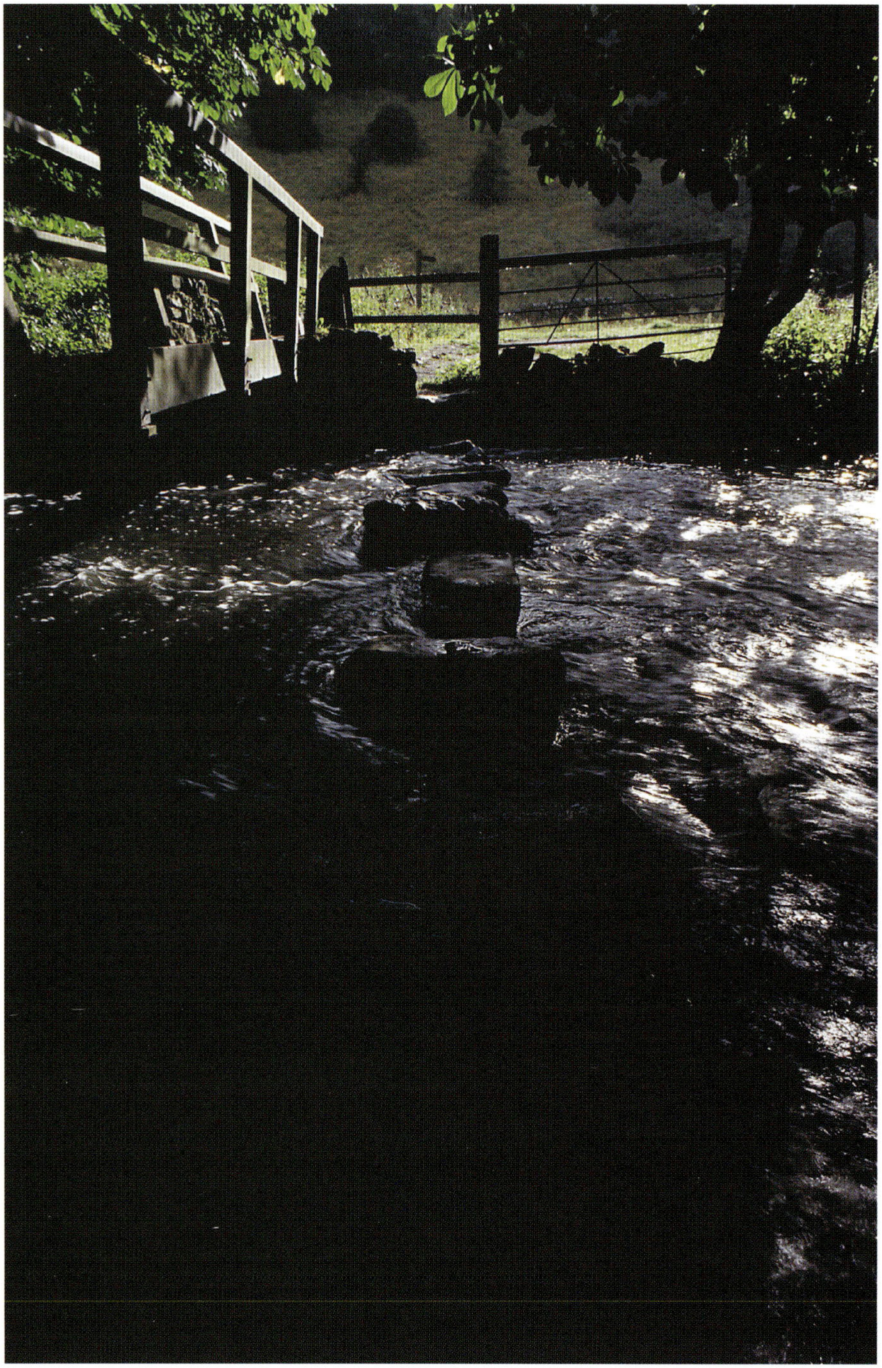

Swaying Bridges

Does the quality of true friendship change?
Do the drips of time erode the key-stones
That link our common walls and crumbling frames?
Do the decades leach strength, as they do with bones?
Do those swaying bridges, that link the banks
Of dividing rivers that 'tween us flow,
Survive the great march of years' serried ranks
Or does the silt make strong foundations grow?
Will we, forever, tip-toe 'cross the spans
That lie above both raging torrents and small streams
And meet and, warmly, shake each other's hand,
And speak of lasting friendship and our dreams?
May those old, swaying bridges long endure;
May their chains and foundations stay secure.

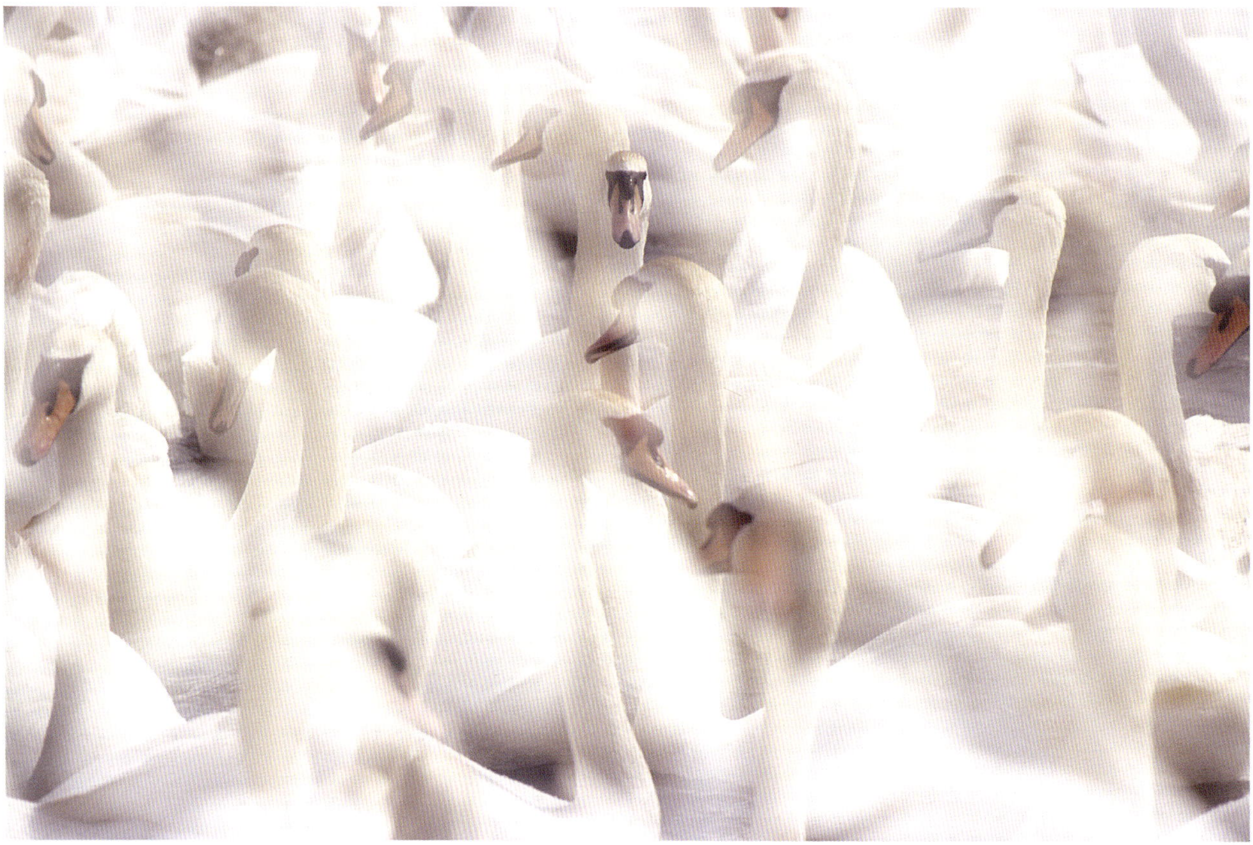

Pictures in the Mist

Farewell, my friend, I fear I must leave you.
I need to go where the old mute swans glide.
I must retire to banks where the sun shines through,
And where trailing fingers of willows hide.
I need to float in warm rivers of peace;
To hear the lap of waves; the drone of flies.
I need to wallow in that warm release;
That gold, as light on the horizon dies.
I need to stretch out like a tired, old dog.
Across the hearths of dancing, winter fires;
To gaze into the mists and autumn fogs
And see the pictures that my life inspired.
But, fear not, I will not forget your face.
In my dreams, it will have a special place.

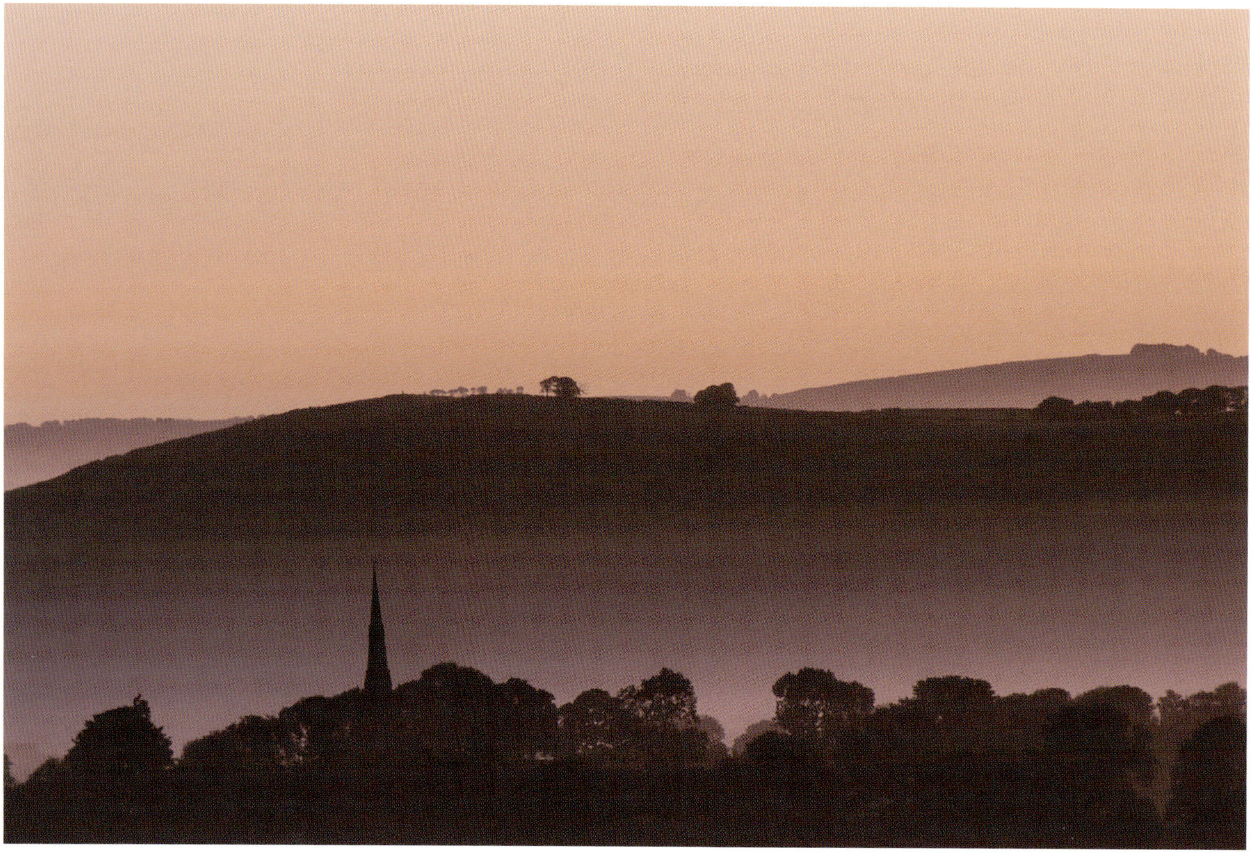

Distant Summits

True friendship
Is like a distant mountain peak:
It is there.
Even in the foothills of uncertainty.
It may not be visible
From the valleys of despair
But it is there , always.
It is a towering rock
That has weathered
A thousand storms;
Solid, proud and immovable.
It is a shining summit,
To be scaled with mutual respect,
Not in domination or conquest,
But in warm enjoyment.
On the coldest of winter afternoons,
It shines, golden, in the sun;
After the blackest night,
It is there,
Silent and majestic,
Awaiting to greet each new dawn.
It is a reassuring, familiar silhouette
On Life's horizons:
Noble, silent yet never understated.
It is just there!

Poem and Image Notes

Brief notes on each of the poems are followed (in italics)
by notes on the accompanying photographs.

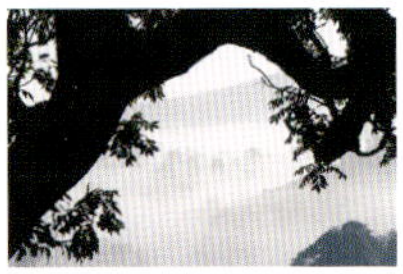

Dawning Light

I started to write poetry late in life. I nailed my colours to the mast in my quest to sail the seas of destiny and to display my simplistic philosophy – for a middle-aged man, a dawning light !

Butterton Clews, Peak District
The ethereal mists of a typical early Autumn morning with the treetops slowly emerging in the valley.

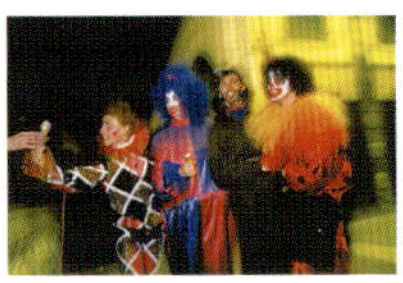

Invitation to the Dance

An emotive allegoric poem written to my wife for our wedding anniversary.

Venice
These colourful carnival revelers were enjoying themselves.

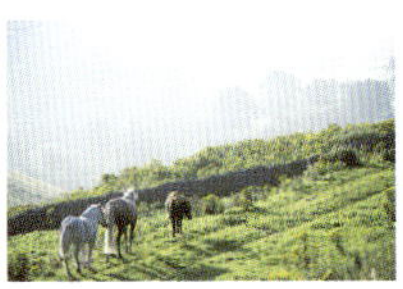

Summer Meadows

A poetic reminiscence of my boyhood days in Derbyshire and in the islands of rural peace in the suburbs of an expanding county town.

Earl Sterndale, Peak District
Early morning meadow.

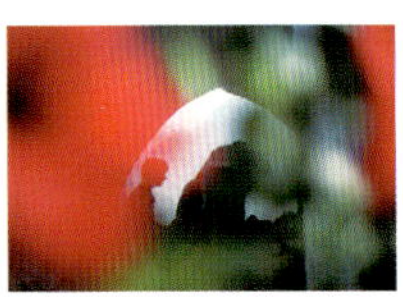

Ambience

Shared meals in good company are good food for the soul!

Binibeca, Minorca
Friends talking during a quiet moment, seen through an arch.

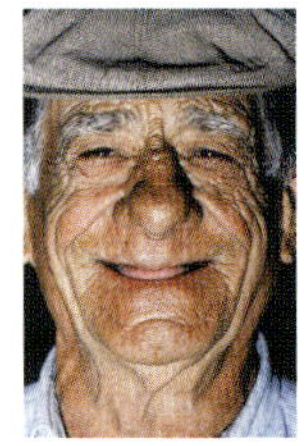

Freundschaft

A poem written after a pleasant holiday in the Vogelsberg, a lovely rural part of Germany, east of Frankfurt.

Silves, Algarve
This old fisherman wasn't sure about being photographed, until I mimicked a smile at him, by pulling at the sides of my mouth.

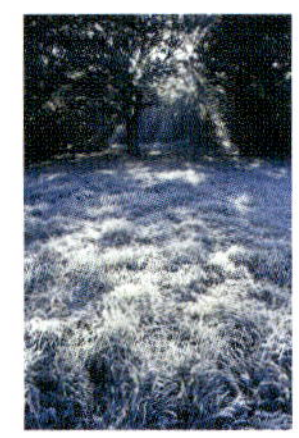

Let Sleeping Dogs Lie

Sentimental piece of rhyme which may strike a chord with those who have loved and lost a loyal pet.

Ashtead Park, Surrey
The frost lying on the grass dappled by the sun through the trees.

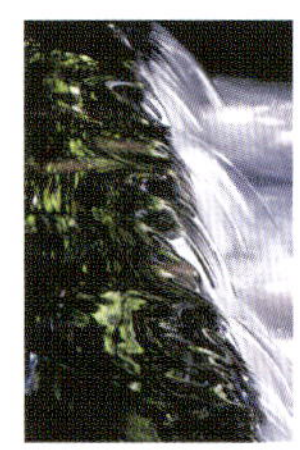

Rivers of Memories

A mellow Sonnet, inspired by a late Autumn walk as part of a reunion with old school friends.

Beresford Dale, Peak District
Looking like glass, water falling over stone reflecting overhead leaves.

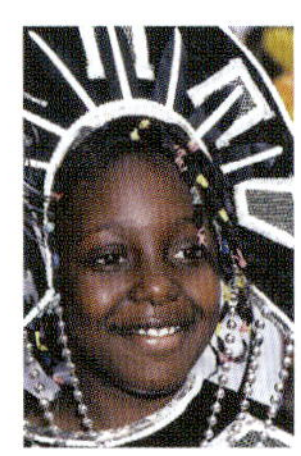

Anatomy of a smile

A soliloquy written after observing a young woman on a crowded commuter train reading an evidently amusing book and her unselfconscious smiles of pleasure.

Notting Hill, London
This beautiful young girl was enjoying herself, just as I was, at the Carnival.

Poem and Image Notes

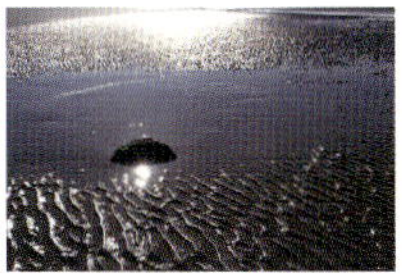

Tears in the Sand

A lasting tribute to my late friend Keith who was tragically drowned off the Norfolk Coast. I used the allegory of the poet Shelley's death by drowning in the Bay of Spezia in 1826. Shelley had an heroic funeral pyre on the beach, witnessed by Byron and other literary figures. His remains were interred in Rome and he passed into the annals of history.

Camber Sands, Sussex
The rising sun reflected in the wet sand at low tide.

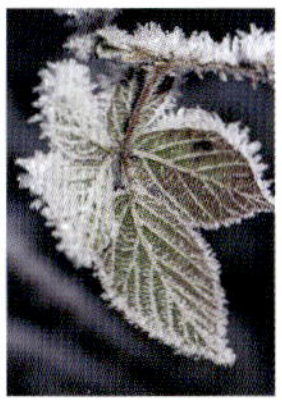

Reflections on a Wet Autumn Day

An elegy also to my friend Keith, describing my paralysis by grief at his funeral service and my anguish that I had not made better use of our lasting boyhood friendship.

Ashtead Park, Surrey
A true autumnal feeling of frost on bramble leaves glittering in the sun.

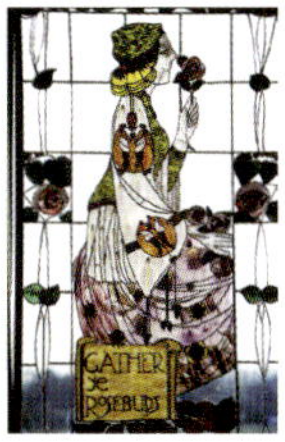

Cherished Memories

A reflective poem written to the memory of my Aunt Olive, the last survivor of my father's generation.

Flower-arranging exhibition, Denbies Vineyard, Dorking
A window painted using materials derived from plants.

Summer Tides

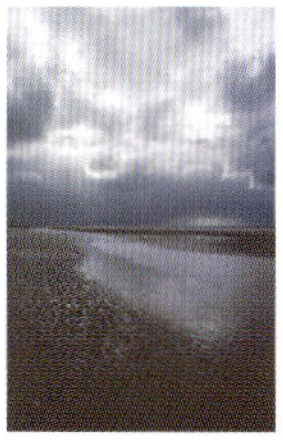

My wife and I shared a difficult problem for nearly a decade. This poem reflects that tranquility and companionship when we could forget our burdens.

Camber Sands, Sussex
Stormy skies over the patterns left by a receding tide.

Attributes of Love

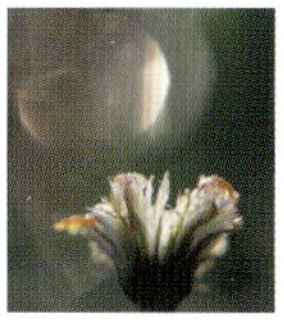

A love sonnet, written to my wife, Beryl, to celebrate 35 years of our marriage.

Ashtead Park, Surrey
Early morning dew on a flower, with sunlight dappling the pond behind.

Willow

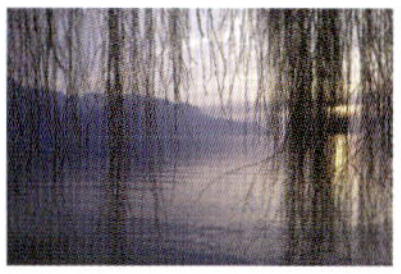

A sonnet composed for a tall, elegant lady colleague, retiring from the Health Service.

Lake Lucerne, Switzerland
Sunset over the lake, through the drooping boughs.

Games of Life

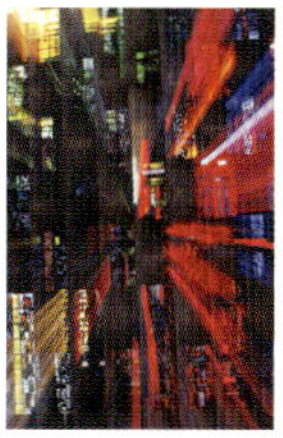

How chance plays its part in enduring friendship.

John Piper window, Coventry Cathedral
A double exposure that evokes the feeling of awe that this wonderful stained glass creates.

Poem and Image Notes

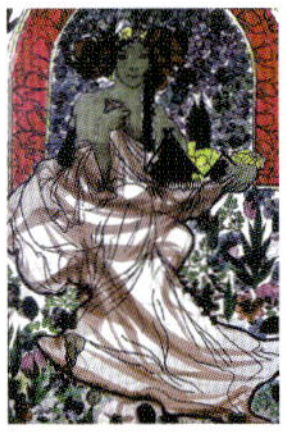

Concern

A sonnet written to a friend, a senior Nurse, who had spent much of her life counseling cancer patients and discovered she had the same disease.

Flower-arranging exhibition, Denbies Vineyard, Dorking
Another simulated stained glass window from the same exhibition.

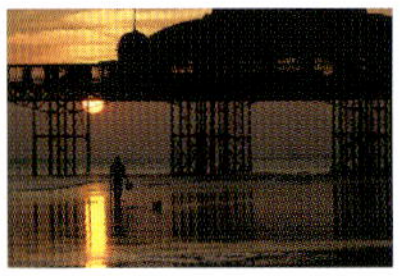

Dolphin Schools

I wrote these fourteen lines for another colleague to show that I, and all of her friends at work, would support her through difficult times.

Brighton
Taken at sunset before the Old Pier was burnt down.

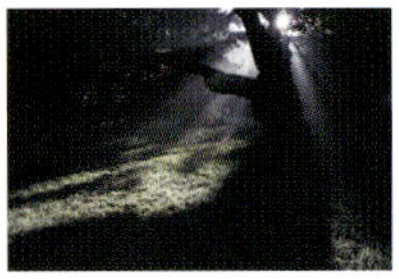

Lighthouse Keepers

A tribute to a wonderful and courageous lady patient, whom I had known for nearly three decades.

Ashtead Park, Surrey
Early morning light pointing the way.

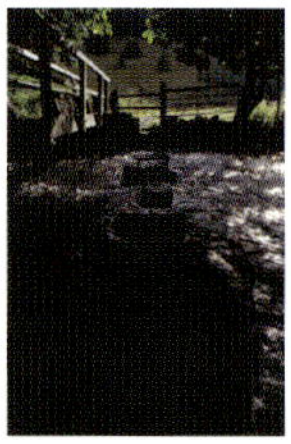

Swaying Bridges

A sonnet about tenuous but long-standing friendships, in this case, a fellow student with whom I had lost touch until chance reunited us.

Beresford Dale, Peak District
Ramblers Bridge and Stepping Stones over the Dove.

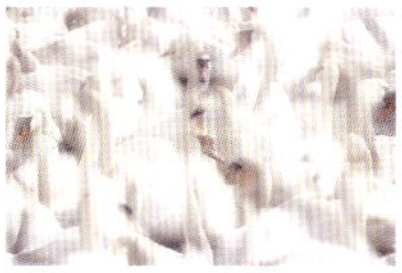

Pictures in the Mist

A reflective sonnet written to each of my friends on the occasion of my retirement.

Abbotsbury Swannery, Dorset
A double exposure taken when the swans gather to feed.

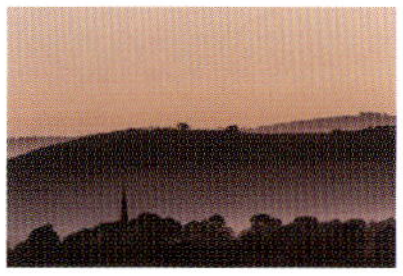

Distant Summits

Inspired by the distant view of Mount Kenya.

Butterton, Peak District
The church tower standing out above early morning mist.